Making Money in

Trading

I0473148

Trade Finance

Guide

By

Patrick W. Nee

The Internationalist

www.internationalist.com

Other Titles Featured in the Business Guides Series

MAKING MONEY IN CHINA: Key Business Contacts and Addresses

MAKING MONEY IN CHINA: China Business Guide and Contacts

MAKING MONEY IN CHINA: China Country Guide for Businesses

MAKING MONEY IN RUSSIA: Russia Country Guide for Businesses

MAKING MONEY IN EXPORTING: A Complete Guide to the Business of Exporting

MAKING MONEY IN Brazil: Brazil Business Guide and Contacts

<u>**The Internationalist**</u>®

International Business, Investment, and Travel

Published by:
The Internationalist Publishing Company
96 Walter Street/Suite 200
Boston MA 02131, USA
Tel: 617-354-7722
www.internationalist.com
PN@internationalist.com

Welcome to the **Internationalist Business Guides** series:

The key to a successful business is knowing the market. MAKING MONEY IN TRADING: TRADE FINANCE GUIDE offers business owners, investors, and entrepreneurs all the need-to-know information to succeed in the field.

Written as an in-depth, straightforward reference guide, this book lists key information about financing trades. Readers will find information about the various methods, their pros and cons, and managing risk.

MAKING MONEY IN TRADING: TRADE FINANCE GUIDE is an instructive manual for those who want to expand their business—or start a new one—by trading.

Whether you are looking to break into international business or need to update your knowledge on modern-day trading procedures, this comprehensive guide is for you.

The Internationalist

Contents

Chapter 1: Overview

The United States is the world's largest exporter, with $1.5 trillion in goods and services exported annually. In 2006, the United States was the top exporter of services and second largest exporter of goods, behind only Germany. However, 95 percent of the world's consumers live outside of the United States. So if you are selling only domestically, you are reaching just a small share of potential customers. Exporting enables SMEs to diversify their portfolios and insulates them against periods of slower growth in the domestic economy.

Free trade agreements have opened in numerous markets including Australia, Canada, Chile, Israel, Jordan, Mexico, and Singapore, as well as Central America. Free trade agreements create more opportunities for U.S. businesses. The Trade Finance Guide is designed to provide U.S. SMEs with the knowledge necessary to grow and become competitive in foreign markets.

Methods of Payment in International Trade

To succeed in today's global marketplace and win sales against foreign competitors, exporters must offer their customers attractive sales terms supported by appropriate payment methods. Because getting paid in full and on time is the ultimate goal for each export sale, an appropriate payment method must be chosen carefully to minimize the payment risk while also accommodating the needs of the buyer.

There are four primary methods of payment for international transactions. During or beforecontract negotiations, you should consider which method in the figure is mutually desir-
able for both you and your customer.

To succeed in today's global market place and win sales against international trade presents a spectrum of risk, which causes uncertainty over the timing of payments between the exporter (seller) and importer (foreign buyer). For exporters, any sale is a gift until payment is received. Therefore, exporters want to receive payment as soon as possible, preferably as soon as an order is placed or before the goods are sent to the importer.

For importers, any payment is a donation until the goods are received. Therefore, importers want to receive the goods as soon as possible but to delay payment as long as possible, preferably until after the goods are resold to generate enough income to pay the exporter.

Cash-in-Advance

With cash-in-advance payment terms, the exporter can avoid credit risk because payment is received before the ownership of the goods is transferred. Wire transfers and credit cards are the most commonly used cash-in-advance options available to exporters. However, requiring payment in advance is the least attractive option for the buyer, because it creates cash-flow problems. Foreign buyers are also concerned that the goods may not be sent if payment is made in advance. Thus, exporters who insist on this payment method as their sole manner of doing business may lose to competitors who offer more attractive payment terms.

Letters of Credit

Letters of credit (LCs) are one of the most secure instruments available to international traders. An LC is a commitment by a bank on behalf of the buyer that payment will be made to the exporter, provided that the terms and conditions stated in the LC have been met, as verified through the presentation of all required documents. The buyer pays his or her bank to render this service. An LC is useful when reliable credit information about a foreign buyer is difficult to obtain, but the exporter is satisfied with the creditworthiness of the buyer's foreign bank. An LC also protects the buyer because no payment obligation arises until the goods have been shipped or delivered as promised.

Documentary Collections

A documentary collection (D/C) is a transaction whereby the exporter entrusts the collection of a payment to the remitting bank (exporter's bank), which sends documents to a collecting bank (importer's bank), along with instructions for payment. Funds are received from the importer and remitted to the exporter through the banks involved in the collection in exchange for those documents. D/Cs involve using a draft that requires the importer to pay the face amount either at sight (document against payment) or on a specified date (document against acceptance). The draft gives instructions that specify the documents required for the transfer of title to the goods. Although banks do act as facilitators for their clients, D/Cs offer no verification process and limited recourse in the event of non-pay- ment. Drafts are generally less expensive than LCs.

Open Account

An open account transaction is a sale where the goods are shipped and delivered before payment is due, which is usually in 30 to 90 days. Obviously, this option is the most advantageous option to the importer in terms of cash flow and cost, but it is consequently the highest risk option for an exporter. Because of intense competition in export markets, foreign buyers often press exporters for open account terms since the extension of credit by the seller to the buyer is more common abroad. Therefore, exporters who are reluctant to extend credit may lose a sale to their competitors. However, the exporter can offer competitive open account terms while substantially mitigating the risk of non-payment by using of one or more of the appropriate trade finance techniques, such as export credit insurance.

Chapter 2: Cash-in-Advance

With the cash-in-advance payment method, the exporter can avoid credit risk or the risk of non-payment since payment is received prior to the transfer of ownership of the goods. Wire transfers and credit cards are the most commonly used cash-in-advance options available to exporters.

However, requiring payment in advance is the least attractive option for the buyer, because it tends to create cash-flow problems, and it often is not a competitive option for the exporter especially when the buyer has other vendors to choose from. In addition, foreign buyers are often concerned that the characteristics ofgoods may not be sent if payment is made in advance.

Full or significant partial payment is required, usu-ally through a credit card or a bank or wire transfer, before the ownership of the goods is transferred. Cash-in-advance, especially a wire transfer, is the most secure and favorable method of international trading for exporters and, consequently, the least secure and attractive method for importers. However, both the credit risk and the competitive landscape must be considered.

Insisting on cash-in-advance could, ultimately, cause exporters to lose customers to competitors who are willing to offer more favorable payment terms to foreign buyers.

Creditworthy foreign buyers, who prefer greater security and better cash utilization, may find cash in-advance unacceptable and simply walk away from the deal.

Risk:
Exporter is exposed to virtually no risk as the burden of risk is placed nearly completely on the importer.

Pros:
Payment before shipment
 Eliminates risk of non-payment

Cons:
May lose customers to competitors over
 payment terms
No additional earnings through financing
 operations

Wire Transfer: Most Secure and Preferred Cash-in-Advance Method

An international wire transfer is commonly used and is almost immediate. Exporters should provide clear routing instructions to the importer when using this method, including the receiving bank's name and address, SWIFT (Society for Worldwide Interbank Financial Telecommunication) address, and ABA (American Banking Association) number, as well as the seller's name and address, bank account title, and account number. This option is more costly to the importer than other cash-in-advance options as the fee for an international wire transfer is usually paid by the sender.

Credit Card: A Viable Cash-in-Advance Method

Exporters who sell directly to foreign buyers may select credit cards as a viable cash-in-advance option, especially for consumer goods or small transactions. Exporters should check with their credit card companies for specific rules on international use of credit cards. The rules governing international credit card transactions differ from those for domestic use. Because international credit card transactions are typically placed using the Web, telephone, or fax, which facilitate fraudulent transactions, proper precautions should be taken to determine the validity of transactions before the goods are shipped. Although exporters must endure the fees charged by credit card companies and take the risk of unfounded disputes, credit cards may help business grow because of their convenience.

Payment by Check: A Less-Attractive Cash-in-Advance Method

Advance payment using an international check may result in a lengthy collection delay of several weeks to months. Therefore, this method may defeat the original intention of receiving payment before shipment. If the check is in U.S. dollars and drawn on a U.S. bank, the collection process is the same as for any U.S. check. However, funds deposited by non-local checks, especially those totaling more than $5,000 on any one day, may not become available for withdrawal for up to 10 business days due to Regulation CC of the Federal Reserve (§ 229.13 (ii)). In addition, if the check is in a foreign currency or drawn on a foreign bank, the collection process can become more complicated and can significantly delay the availability of funds. Moreover, if shipment is made before the check is collected, there is a risk that the check may be returned due to insufficient funds in the buyer's account or even because of a stop-payment order.

When to Use Cash-in-Advance Terms

The importer is a new customer and/or has a less-established operating history. The importer's creditworthiness is doubtful, unsatisfactory, or unverifiable. The political and commercial risks of the importer's home country are very high. The exporter's product is unique, not available elsewhere, or in heavy demand. The exporter operates an Internet-based business where the acceptance of credit card payments is a must to remain competitive.

Chapter 3: Letters of Credit

Letters of credit (LCs) are one of the most secure instruments available to international traders. An LC is a commitment by a bank on behalf of the buyer that payment will be made to the beneficiary (exporter) provided that the terms and conditions stated in the LC have been met, consisting of the presentation of specified documents.

The buyer pays his bank to render this service. An LC is useful when reliable credit information about a foreign buyer is difficult to obtain, but the exporter is satisfied with the creditworthiness of the buyer's foreign bank. This method also protects the buyer since the documents required to trigger payment provide evidence that the goods have been shipped or delivered as promised. However, because LCs have many opportunities for discrepancies, documents should be prepared by well-trained professionals or outsourced. Discrepant documents, literally not having an "i dotted and t crossed," can negate the bank's payment obligation.with the creditworthiness of the buyer's bank.

An LC, also referred to as a documentary credit, is a contractual agreement whereby the issuing bank (importer's bank), acting on behalf of its customer (the buyer or importer), authorizes the nominated bank (exporter's bank), to make payment to the beneficiary or exporter against the receipt of stipulated documents.

The LC is a separate contract from the sales contract on which it is based; therefore, the bank is not concerned whether each party fulfills the terms of the sales contract. The bank's obligation to pay is solely conditioned upon the seller's compliance with the terms and conditions of the LC. In LC transactions, banks deal in documents only, not goods. LCs can be arranged easily for one-time deals. Unless the conditions of the LC state otherwise, it is always irrevocable, which means the document may not be changed or cancelled unless the seller agrees.

Risk:
Risk is evenly spread between seller and buyer, provided that all terms and conditions are adhered to.

Pros:
Payment made after shipment
A variety of payment, financing, and risk mitigation options available

Cons:
Complex and labor-intensive process
Relatively expensive method in terms of transaction costs

Confirmed Letter of Credit

A greater degree of protection is afforded to the exporter when an LC issued by a foreign bank (the importer's issuing bank) is confirmed by a U.S. bank and the exporter asks its customer to have the issuing bank authorize a bank in the exporter's country to confirm (the advising bank, which then becomes the confirming bank). This confirmation means that the U.S. bank adds its engagement to pay the exporter to that of the foreign bank. If an LC is not confirmed, the exporter is subject to the payment risk of the foreign bank and the political risk of the importing country. Exporters should consider getting confirmed LCs if they are concerned about the credit standing of the foreign bank or when they are operating in a high-risk market, where political upheaval, economic collapse, devaluation or exchange controls could put the payment at risk.

Illustrative Letter of Credit Transaction

1. The importer arranges for the issuing bank to open an LC in favor of the exporter.

2. The issuing bank transmits the LC to the nominated bank, which forwards it to the exporter.

3. The exporter forwards the goods and documents to a freight forwarder.

4. The freight forwarder dispatches the goods and submits documents to the nominated bank.

5. The nominated bank checks documents for compliance with the LC and collects payment from the issuing bank for the exporter.

6. The importer's account at the issuing bank is debited.

7. The issuing bank releases documents to the importer to claim the goods from the carrier and to clear them at customs.

Special Letters of Credit

LCs can take many forms. When an LC is made transferable, the payment obligation under the original LC can be transferred to one or more "second beneficiaries." With a revolving LC, the issuing bank restores the credit to its original amount each time it is drawn down. A standby LC is not intended to serve as the means of payment for goods but can be drawn in the event of a contractual default, including the failure of an importer to pay invoices when due. Standby LCs are often posted by exporters in favor of importers as well because they can serve as bid bonds, performance bonds, and advance payment guarantees. In addition, standby LCs are often used as counter guarantees against the provision of down payments and progress payments on the part of foreign buyers. A buyer may object to a seller's request for a standby LC for two reasons: it ties up a portion of the seller's line of credit and it is costly.

Tips for Exporters

1. Consult with your bank before the importer applies for an LC. Consider whether a confirmed LC is needed.

2. Negotiate with the importer and agree on detailed terms to be incorporated into the LC.

3. Determine if all LC terms can be met within the prescribed time limits.

4. Ensure that all the documents are consistent with the terms and conditions of the LC.

5. Beware of many discrepancy opportunities that may cause non-payment or delayed payment

Chapter 4: Documentary Collections

A documentary collection (D/C) is a transaction whereby the exporter entrusts the collection of a payment to the remitting bank (exporter's bank), which sends documents to a collecting bank (importer's bank), along with instructions for payment.

Funds are received from the importer and remitted to the exporter through the banks in exchange for those documents. D/Cs involve using a draft that requires the importer to pay the face amount either at sight (document against payment [D/P] or cash against documents) or on a specified date (document against acceptance [D/A] or cash against acceptance). The draft gives instructions that specify the documents required for the transfer of title to the goods.

Although banks do act as facilitators for their clients under collections, D/Cs offer no verification process and limited recourse in the event of non-payment. Drafts are generally less expensive than letters of credit (LCs).relationships and in stable export markets.

D/Cs are less complicated and less expensive than LCs. Under a D/C transaction, the importer is not obligated to pay for goods before shipment. The exporter retains the title to the goods until the importer either pays the face amount at sight or accepts the draft to incur a legal obligation to pay at a specified later date. Although the title to the goods can be controlled under ocean shipments, it cannot be controlled under air and overland shipments, which allow the foreign buyer to receive the goods with or without payment. The remitting bank (exporter's bank) and the collecting bank (importer's bank) play an essential role in D/Cs.

Risk:

Riskier for the exporter, though D/C terms are more convenient and cheaper than an LC to the importer.

Pros:

Bank assistance in obtaining payment

The process is simple, fast, and less costly than LCs

Cons

Banks' role is limited and they do not guarantee payment

Banks do not verify the accuracy of the documents

Although the banks control the flow of documents, they neither verify the documents nor take any risks. They can, however, influence the mutually satisfactory settlement of a D/C transaction.

When to Use Documentary Collections

With D/Cs, the exporter has little recourse against the importer in case of non-payment. Thus, D/Cs should be used only under the following conditions: The exporter and importer have a well-established relationship. The exporter is confident that the importing country is politically and economically stable. An open account sale is considered too risky, and an LC is unacceptable to the importer.

Typical Simplified D/C Transaction Flow

1. The exporter ships the goods to the importer and receives the documents in exchange.

2. The exporter presents the documents with instructions for obtaining payment to his bank.

3. The exporter's remitting bank sends the documents to the importer's collecting bank.

4. The collecting bank releases the documents to the importer on receipt of payment or acceptance of the draft.

5. The importer uses the documents to obtain the goods and to clear them at customs.

6. Once the collecting bank receives payment, it forwards the proceeds to the remitting bank.

7. The remitting bank then credits the exporter's account.

Documents against Payment Collection

With a D/P collection, the exporter ships the goods and then gives the documents to his bank, which will forward the documents to the importer's collecting bank, along with instructions on how to collect the money from the importer. In this arrangement, the collecting bank releases the documents to the importer only on payment for the goods. Once payment is received, the collecting bank transmits the funds to the remitting bank for payment to the exporter.

Documents Against Acceptance Collection

With a D/A collection, the exporter extends credit to the importer by using a time draft. The documents are released to the importer to claim the goods upon his signed acceptance of the time draft. By accepting the draft, the importer becomes legally obligated to pay at a specific date. At maturity, the collecting bank contacts the importer for payment. Upon receipt of payment, the collecting bank transmits the funds to the remitting bank for payment to the exporter.

Chapter 5: Open Account

An open account transaction is a sale where the goods are shipped and delivered before payment is due, which is usually in 30 to 90 days. Obviously, this option is the most advantageous to the importer in terms of cash flow and cost, but it is consequently the highest-risk option for an exporter. Because of intense competition in export markets, foreign buyers often press exporters for open account terms.

In addition, the extension of credit by the seller to the buyer is more common abroad. Therefore, exporters who are reluctant to extend credit may lose a sale to their competitors. However, though open account terms will definitely enhance export competitiveness, exporters should thoroughly examine the political, economic, and commercial risks as well as cultural influences to ensure that payment will be received in full and on time.

It is possible to substantially mitigate the risk of non-payment with open account trade by using such trade finance techniques as export credit insurance and factoring.more appropriate trade finance techniques. Exporters may also seek export working capital financing to ensure that they have access to financing for production and for credit while waiting for payment.

The goods, along with all the necessary documents, are shipped directly to the importer who has agreed to pay the exporter's invoice at a specified date which is usually in 30 to 90 days. The exporter should be absolutely confident that the importer will accept shipment and pay at the agreed time and that the importing country is commercially and politically secure. Open account terms may help win customers in competitive markets and may be used with one or more of the appropriate trade finance techniques that mitigate the risk of non-payment.

Pros
Boosts competitiveness in the global market
Helps establish and maintain a successful trade relationship

Cons
Significant exposure to the risk of non-payment
Additional costs associated with risk mitigation measures

How to Offer Open Account Terms in Competitive Markets

Open account terms may be offered in competitive markets with the use of one or more of the following trade finance techniques: (a) export working capital financing, (b) government-guaranteed export working capital programs, (c) export credit insurance, and (d) export factoring.

Export Working Capital Financing

Exporters who lack sufficient funds to extend open accounts in the global market needs export working capital financing that covers the entire cash cycle, the from purchase of raw materials through the ultimate collection of the sales proceeds. Export working capital facilities, which are generally secured by personal guarantees, assets, or receivables, can be structured to support export sales in the form of a loan or a revolving line of credit.

Government-Guaranteed Export Working Capital Programs: The U.S. Small Business Administration and the Export–Import Bank of the United States offer programs that guarantee export working capital facilities granted by participating lenders to U.S. exporters. With those programs, U.S. exporters can obtain needed facilities from commercial lenders when financing is otherwise not available or when borrowing capacity needs to be increased.

Export Credit Insurance:

Export credit insurance provides protection against commercial losses (such as default, insolvency, and bankruptcy) and political losses (such as war, nationalization, and currency inconvertibility). It allows exporters to increase sales by offering liberal open account terms to new and existing customers. Insurance also provides security for banks that are providing working capital and are financing exports.

Export Factoring:

Factoring in international trade is the discounting of short-term receivables (up to 180 days). The exporter transfers title to short-term foreign accounts receivable to a factoring house, or a factor, for cash at a discount from the face value. It allows an exporter to ship on open account as the factor assumes the financial ability of the importer to pay and handles collections on the receivables. The factoring house usually works with exports of consumer goods.

Trade Finance Technique Unavailable for Open Account Terms:

Forfaiting:

Forfaiting is a method of trade financing that allows the exporter to sell medium-term receivables (180 days to 7 years) to the forfaiter at a discount, in exchange for cash. The forfaiter assumes all the risks, thereby enabling the exporter to offer extended credit terms and to incorporate the discount into the selling price. Forfaiters usually work with exports of capital goods, commodities, and large projects.

Forfaiting was developed in Switzerland in the 1950s to fill the gap between the exporter of capital goods, who would not or could not deal on open account, and the importer, who desired to defer payment until the capital equipment could begin to pay for itself.

Chapter 6: Export Working Capital Financing

Export working capital (EWC) financing allows exporters to purchase the goods and services they need to support their export sales. More specifically, EWC facilities extended by commercial lenders provide a means for small and medium-sized enterprises (SMEs) that lack sufficient internal liquidity to process and acquire goods and services to fulfill export orders and to extend open account terms to their foreign buyers.

EWC funds are commonly used to finance three different areas: (a) materials, (b) labor, and (c) inventory, but they can also be used to finance receivables generated from export sales and/or standby letters of credit used as performance bonds or payment guarantees to foreign buyers. An unexpected large export order or many incremental export orders can place challenging demands on working capital. EWC financing, which is generally secured by personal guarantees, assets, or high-value accounts receivable, helps to ease and stabilize cash-flow problems of exporters while they fulfill export sales and grow competitively in the global market.

Funds may be used to acquire materials, labor, inventory, goods, and services for export. A facility can support a single export transaction (transaction-specific short-term loan) or multiple export transactions (revolving line of credit) on open account terms. A transaction-specific loan is generally up to one year, and a revolving line of credit may extend up to three years. Availability is generally limited to financially-stable large corporations or established SMEs with access to strong personal guarantees, assets, or high-value accounts receivable. A government guarantee may be needed to obtain a facility that can meet export needs. Significant risk of non-payment for exporter unless proper risk mitigation measures are used.

Pros:
Allows fulfillment of export sales orders
Allows exporter to offer open account terms to remain competitive

Cons:
Generally available only to SMEs with access to strong personal guarantees, assets, or high-value receivables
Additional costs associated with risk mitigation measures
Exporters may need risk mitigation to offer open account terms confidently in the global market.

Where and How to Obtain an Export Working Capital Facility

Many commercial banks and lenders offer facilities for export activities. To qualify, exporters generally need (a) to be in business profitably for at least 12 months (not necessarily in exporting), (b) to demonstrate a need for transaction-based financing, and (c) to provide documents to demonstrate that a viable transaction exists. Note that personal guarantees, collateral assets, or high-value accounts receivable are generally required for SMEs to obtain commercial EWC facilities. The lender may place alien on the exporter's assets, such as inventory and accounts receivable, to ensure repayment of a loan. In addition, all export sales proceeds will usually be collected by the lender before the balance is passed on to the exporter. Fees and interest rates are usually negotiable between the lender and the exporter.

Short-Term Loans or Revolving Lines of Credit

Basically, there are two types of EWC facilities: transaction-specific short-term loans and revolving lines of credit. Short-term loans, which are appropriate for large and periodic export orders, are typically if the outflows and inflows of funds are predictable over time.

Short-term loans can be contracted for 3, 6, 9, or 12 months, and the interest rates are usually fixed over the requested tenors. Revolving lines of credit, however, are appropriate for a series of small export orders because they are designed to cover temporary funding needs that cannot always be anticipated. Revolving lines of credit have a very flexible structure so that exporters can draw funds against current account at any time and up to a specified limit.

Why a Government Guarantee May Be Needed

The U.S. Small Business Administration and the Export–Import Bank of the United States offer programs that guarantee EWC facilities to U.S. exporters. These programs allow U.S. exporters to obtain needed facilities from participating lenders when commercial financing is otherwise not available or when their borrowing capacity needs to be increased.

Advance rates offered by commercial banks on export inventory and foreign account receivables are not always sufficient to meet the needs of exporters. In addition, some lenders do not lend to exporters without a government guarantee due to repayment risks associated with export sales.

Why Risk Mitigation May Be Needed

Although EWC financing certainly makes it possible for exporters to offer open account terms in today's highly competitive global markets, the use of such financing does not necessarily eliminate the risk of non-payment by foreign customers. Some forms of risk mitigation may be needed in order to offer open account terms more confidently in the global market and to obtain EWC financing. For example, a lender may require an exporter to obtain export credit insurance as a condition of providing working capital and financing exports.

Chapter 7: Government-Guaranteed Export

Working Capital Loan Programs

Financing offered by commercial lenders on export inventory and foreign accounts receivables is not always sufficient to meet the needs of U.S. exporters. Early-stage small and medium-sized exporters are usually not eligible for commercial financing without a government guarantee. In addition, commercial lenders are generally reluctant to extend credit due to the repayment risk associated with export sales. In such cases, government-guaranteed export working capital (EWC) loans can provide the exporter with the liquidity to accept new business, can help grow U.S. export sales, and can let U.S. firms compete more effectively in the global marketplace.

Two U.S. government agencies—the U.S. Small Business Administration (SBA) and the Export–Import Bank of the United States (Ex–Im Bank)—offer loan guarantees to participating lenders for making export loans to U.S. businesses. Both agencies focus on export trade financing, with SBA typically handling facilities up to $2 million and Ex–Im Bank processing facilities of all sizes. Through government-guaranteed EWC loans, U.S. exporters can obtain financing from participating lenders when commercial financing is otherwise not available or when their borrowing needs are greater than the lenders' credit standards would allow.

The loan expands access to EWC for supplier financing and production costs. The loan maximizes the borrowing base by turning export inventory and accounts receivable into cash. Risk mitigation may be needed to offer open account terms confidently in the global market. SBA's EWC loan is appropriate for U.S. small-sized businesses and has credit lines up to $2 million. Ex–Im Bank's EWC loan is available to all U.S. businesses, including small and medium-sized exporters, and has credit lines of all sizes.

Pros:
Encourages lenders to offer financing to exporters
Enables lenders to offer generous advance rates

Cons:
Cost of obtaining and maintaining a guaranteed facility
Additional costs associated with risk mitigation measures

Key Features of the SBA's Export Working Capital Program

1. Exporters must meet SBA eligibility and size standards.
2. There is no application fee and no restrictions regarding foreign content or military sales.
3. A 0.25 percent upfront facility fee is based on the guaranteed portion of a loan of 12 months or fewer.

4. Fees and interest rates charged by the commercial lender are negotiable.

5. The "Export Express" pilot program can provide exporters and lenders a streamlined method to obtain SBA-backed financing for EWC loans of up to $250,000. With an expedited eligibility review, a response may be obtained in fewer than 24 hours.

Key Features of Ex–Im Bank's Export Working Capital Program

1. Exporters must adhere to the Bank's requirements for content, non-nuclear uses, non-military uses, and environmental and economic impact and to the Country Limitation Schedule.

2. There is a non-refundable $100 application fee.

3. A 1.5 percent upfront facility fee is based on the total loan amount and a one-year loan but may be reduced to 1 percent with export credit insurance and if designated requirements are met.

4. Fees and interest rate charged by the commercial lender are usually negotiable.

5. Enhancements are available for minority- or woman-owned, rural and environmental firms.

Why Risk Mitigation May Be Needed

Government guarantees on export loans do not make exporters immune to the risk of non-payment by foreign customers. Rather, the government guarantee provides lenders with an incentive to offer financing by reducing the lender's risk exposure. Exporters may need some form of risk mitigation, such as export credit insurance, to offer open account terms more confidently. U.S. Department of Commerce International Trade Administration 1 SBA encourages the use of American-made products, if feasible. Borrowers must comply with all export control requirements.

Chapter 8: Export Credit Insurance

Export credit insurance (ECI) protects an exporter of products and services against the risk of non-payment by a foreign buyer. In other words, ECI significantly reduces the payment risks associated with doing international business by giving the exporter conditional assurance that payment will be made if the foreign buyer is unable to pay.

Simply put, exporters can protect their foreign receivables against a variety of risks that could result in non-payment by foreign buyers. ECI generally covers commercial risks, such as insolvency of the buyer, bankruptcy, or protracted defaults (slow payment), and revolution. ECI also covers currency inconvertibility, expropriation, and changes in import or export regulations. ECI is offered either on a single-buyer basis or on a portfolio multi-buyer basis for short-term (up to one year)Recommended for use in conjunction with open and medium-term (one to five years) repayment periods.account terms and export working capital financing.

ECI allows exporters to offer competitive open account terms to foreign buyers while minimizing the risk of non-payment. Even creditworthy buyers could default on payment due to circumstances beyond their control. With reduced non-payment risk, exporters can increase export sales, establish market share in emerging and developing countries, and compete more vigorously in the global market. When foreign accounts receivables are insured, lenders are more willing to increase the exporter's borrowing capacity and to offer attractive financing terms.

Risk:

Risk of uncovered portion of the loss shared by exporters, and their claims may be denied in case of non-compliance with requirements specified in the policy.

Pros

Reduces the risk of non-payment by foreign buyers
Offer open account terms safely in the global market

Cons

Cost of obtaining and maintaining an insurance policy
Risk sharing in the form of a deductible (coverage is usually below 100 percent)

Coverage

Short-term ECI, which provides 90 to 95 percent coverage against commercial and political risks that result in buyer payment defaults, typically covers (a) consumer goods, materials, and services up to 180 days, and (b) small capital goods, consumer durables, and bulk commodities up to 360 days. Medium-term ECI, which provides 85 percent coverage of the net contract value, usually covers large capital equipment up to five years. ECI, which is often incorporated into the selling price, should be a proactive purchase exporters already have coverage before a customer becomes a problem.

Where Can I Get Export Credit Insurance?

ECI policies are offered by many private commercial risk insurance companies as well as the Ex–Im Bank, which is the government agency that assists in financing the export of U.S. goods and services to international markets. U.S. exporters are strongly encouraged to shop for a good specialty insurance broker who can help them select the most cost-effective solution for their needs. Reputable, well-established companies that sell commercial ECI policies are easily found on the Internet. You may also buy ECI policies directly from Ex–Im Bank.

Private-Sector Export Credit Insurance

Premiums are individually determined on the basis of risk factors and may be reduced for established and experienced exporters. Most multi-buyer policies cost less than 1 percent of insured sales, whereas the prices of single-buyer policies vary widely due to presumed higher risk.The cost in most cases is significantly less than the fees charged for letters of credit. There are no restrictions regarding foreign content or military sales.

Ex–Im Bank's Export Credit Insurance

Ex–Im Bank customers are advised to refer to the Exposure Fee Advice Tables to deter mine exposure fees (premiums). Coverage is available in riskier emerging foreign markets where private insurers may not operate. Exporters electing an Ex–Im Bank working capital guarantee may receive a 25 percent premium discount on multi-buyer insurance policies. Enhanced support is offered for environmentally beneficial exports. Products must be shipped from the United States and have at least 50 percent U.S. content.

Ex–Im Bank is unable to support military products or purchases made by foreign military entities. Support for exports may be closed or restricted in certain countries for U.S. government policy reasons

Chapter 9: Forfaiting

Forfaiting is a method of trade finance that allows exporters to obtain cash by selling their medium-term foreign accounts receivable at a discount on a "without recourse" basis. A forfaiter is a specialized finance firm or a department in a bank that performs non-recourse export financing through the purchase of medium-term trade receivables. Similar to factoring, forfaiting virtually eliminates the risk of non-payment, once the goods have been delivered to the foreign buyer in accordance with the terms of sale. However, unlike factors, forfaiters typically work with exporters who sell capital goods, commodities, or large projects and needs to offer periods of credit from 180 days to seven years.

In forfaiting, receivables are normally guaranteed by the importer's bank, which allows the exporter to take the transaction off the balance sheet to enhance key financial ratios. The current minimum transaction size for forfaiting is $100,000. In the United States, most users of forfaiting are large established corporations, but small and medium-sized companies are slowly embracing forfaiting as they become more aggressive in seeking financing solutions for countries considered high risk.

Forfaiting eliminates virtually all risk to the exporter, with 100 percent financing of contract value. Exporters can offer medium-term financing in markets where the credit risk would otherwise be too high. Forfaiting generally works with bills of exchange, promissory notes, or a letter of credit. The exporter is normally required to obtain a bank guarantee for the foreign buyer. Financing can be arranged on a one-shot basis in any of the major currencies, usually at a fixed interest rate, but a floating rate option is also available.

Pros:
Eliminates the risk of non-payment by foreign buyers
Offers strong capabilities in emerging and developing markets

Cons:
Cost is often higher than commercial lender financing
Limited to medium-term transactions and those exceeding $100,000
Forfaiting can be used in conjunction with officially supported credits backed by export credit agencies, such as the Export–Import Bank of the United States.

How Forfaiting Works
The exporter approaches a forfaiter before finalizing a transaction's structure. Once the forfaiter commits to the deal and sets the discount rate, the exporter can incorporate the discount into the selling price. The exporter then

accepts a commitment issued by the forfaiter, signs the contract with the importer, and obtains, if required, a guarantee from the importer's bank that provides the documents required to complete the forfaiting. The exporter delivers the goods to the importer and delivers the documents to the forfaiter who verifies them and pays for them as agreed in the commitment. Since this payment is without recourse, the exporter has no further interest in the transaction and it is the forfaiter who must collect the future payments due from the importer.

Cost of Forfaiting

The cost of forfaiting is determined by the rate of discount based on the aggregate of the LIBOR (London inter bank offered rate) rates for the tenor of the receivables and a margin reflecting the risk being sold. The degree of risk varies based on the importing country, the length of the loan, the currency of transaction, and the repayment structure—the higher the risk, the higher the margin and, therefore, the discount rate. However, forfaiting can be more cost-effective than traditional trade finance tools because of many attractive benefits it offers to the exporter.

Three Additional Major Advantages of Forfaiting

Volume: Forfaiting can work on a one-shot deal, without requiring an ongoing volume of business.

Speed: Commitments can be issued within hours or days depending on details and country.

Simplicity: Documentation is usually simple, concise, and straightforward.

Forfaiting Industry Profile

Forfaiting was developed in Switzerland in the 1950s to fill the gap between the exporter of capital goods, who would not or could not deal on open account, and the importer, who desired to defer payment until the capital equipment could begin to pay for itself. Although the number of forfaiting transactions is growing worldwide, industry sources estimate that only 2 percent of world trade is financed through forfeiting. U.S. forfaiting transactions account for only 3 percent of that volume. Forfaiting firms have opened around the world, but the Europeans maintain a hold on the market, including in North America. Although these firms remain few in number in the United States, the innovative financing they provide should not be overlooked as a viable means of export finance for U.S. exporters.

Where to Find a Forfaiter

The Association of Trade & Forfaiting in the Americas, Inc. (ATFA) and the International Forfaiting Association (IFA) are useful sources for locating forfaiters willing to finance exports. ATFA and IFA are associations of financial institutions dedicated to promoting international trade finance through forfaiting. ATFA is located in New York, and its Web site is www.afia-forfaiting.org. IFA is located in Switzerland and its Web site is www.forfaiters.org.

Chapter 10: Government-Assisted Foreign Buyer Financing

International sales of high-value capital goods or services and exports to large-scale projects, which require medium- or long-term financing, often pose special challenges to exporters as commercial lenders may be reluctant to lend large sums to foreign buyers, especially those in developing countries, for extended periods. One viable solution to these challenges is foreign buyer financing offered by the Export–Import Bank of the United States (Ex–Im Bank). As the official U.S. export credit agency, Ex–Im Bank supports the purchases of U.S. goods and services by creditworthy foreign buyers who are unable to obtain financing they need through traditional commercial sources. Ex–Im Bank does not compete with commercial lenders but provides products that fill gaps in trade financing by assuming country and credit risks that the private sector is unable or unwilling to accept. With Ex–Im Bank's foreign buyer financing, U.S. exporters can turn their business opportunities into real transactions and get paid cash on delivery and acceptance of the goods or services.

Government-assisted foreign buyer financing helps turn export opportunities, especially in high-risk emerging markets, into real transactions for large U.S. corporations and established medium-sized companies, as well as for their small business suppliers. Creditworthy foreign buyers can obtain loans needed for purchases of U.S. goods and services, especially high-value capital goods or services and exports to large-scale projects. This type of financing provides direct loans to for eign buyers at a fixed rate or provides guarantees for term financing offered by commercial lenders. Financing is available for medium-term (up to 5 years) and long-term (generally up to 10 years) transactions. Risk is transferred to Ex–Im Bank and to the foreign buyer who is required to make a 15 percent down payment to the exporter.

Pros:
Buyer financing as part of an attractive sales package
Cash payment upon shipment of the goods or services

Cons
Subject to certain restrictions for U.S. government policy reasons
Possible lengthy process of approving financing

Key Common Features of Ex-Im Bank's Loan Guarantees and Direct Loans

Ex–Im Bank assists U.S. exporters by providing direct loans or by guaranteeing commercial loans to creditworthy foreign buyers for purchases of U.S. goods and services. They are generally used to finance the purchase of high-value capital equipment or services or exports to large-scale projects that require medium- or long-term financing. Ex-

Im Bank's foreign buyer financing is also used to finance the purchase of refurbished equipment, software, and certain banking and legal fees, as well as some local costs and expenses.

There is no minimum or maximum limit to the size of the export sale that may be supported by the bank's foreign buyer financing. Ex–Im Bank requires the foreign buyer to make a cash payment to the exporter equal to at least 15 percent of the U.S. supply contract. Repayment terms of up to five years are available for exports of capital goods and services. Transportation equipment and exports to large-scale projects may be eligible for repayment terms up to 10 years (12 to 15 years for certain sectors). Military items are generally not eligible for Ex–Im Bank financing nor are sales to foreign military entities. In addition, goods must meet the bank's foreign content requirements.

Finally, Ex–Im Bank financing may not be available in certain countries and certain terms for U.S. government policy reasons (for more information, see the Country Limitation Schedule posted on the bank's Web site, www.exim.gov, under the "Tools" section).

Key Features of Ex-Im Bank Loan Guarantees

1. Loans are made by commercial banks and guaranteed by Ex–Im Bank.

2. Loans cover 100 percent principal and interest for 85 percent of the U.S. contract price.

3. Interest rates are negotiable, and are usually floating and lower than fixed rates.

4. Loans are fully transferable, can be securitized, and are available in certain foreign currencies.

5. Loans have a faster documentation process with the assistance of commercial banks.

6. Cash payment financing is promoted.

7. There are no U.S. vessel shipping regulations for amounts less than $20 million.

Key Features of Ex-Im Bank Direct Loans

1. Fixed-rate loans are provided directly to creditworthy foreign buyers.

2. Loans support 85 percent of the U.S. contract price.

3. Exporters will be paid in full upon disbursement of a loan to foreign buyers.

4. Generally, the goods must be carried exclusively on U.S. vessels.

5. Loans are best used when the buyer insists on a fixed rate.

Fees

Letter of interest—$100

Preliminary commitment—0.1 of 1 percent of the financed amount up to $25,000

Guarantee commitment—0.125 percent per year on the undisbursed balance of the loan

Direct loan commitment—0.5 percent per year on the undisbursed balance of the loan

Exposure fee—varies, depending on tenor, country risk, and buyer credit risk

Chapter 11: Foreign Exchange Risk Management

Foreign exchange (FX) is a risk factor that is often overlooked by small and medium-sized enterprises (SMEs) that wish to enter, grow, and succeed in the global market place. Although most U.S. SME exporters prefer to sell in U.S. dollars, creditworthy foreign buyers today are increasingly demanding to pay in their local currencies. From the viewpoint of a U.S. exporter who chooses to sell in foreign currencies, FX risk is the exposure to potential financial losses due to devaluation of the foreign currency against the U.S. dollar. Obviously, this exposure can be avoided by insisting on selling only in U.S. dollars.

However, such an approach may result in losing export opportunities to competitors who are willing to accommodate their foreign buyers by selling in their local currencies. This approach could also result in the non-payment by a foreign buyer who may find it impossible to meet U.S. dollar. While coverage for non-payment could be covered by export credit insurance, such "what-if" protection is meaningless if export opportunities are lost in the first place because of the "payment in U.S. dollars only" policy. Selling in foreign currencies, if FX risk is successfully managed or hedged, can be a viable option for U.S. exporters who wish to enter and remain competitive in the global marketplace.

Most foreign buyers generally prefer to trade in their local currencies to avoid FX risk exposure. U.S. SME exporters who choose to trade in foreign currencies can minimize FX exposure by using one of the widely-used FX risk management techniques available in the United States. The volatile nature of the FX market poses a great risk of sudden and drastic FX rate movements, which may cause significantly damaging financial losses from otherwise profitable export sales.

Pros:

Enhances export sales terms to help exporters remain competitive

Reduces non-payment risk because of local currency devaluation

Cons:

Cost of using some FX risk management techniques

Burden of FX risk management

The primary objective of FX risk management is to minimize potential currency losses, not to make a profit from FX rate movements, which are unpredictable and frequent.

FX Risk Management Options

A variety of options are available for reducing short-term FX exposure. The following sections list FX risk management techniques considered suitable for new-to-export U.S. SME companies. The FX instruments mentioned below are available in all major currencies and are offered by numerous commercial lenders. However, not all of these techniques may be available in the buyer's country or they may be too expensive to be useful.

Non-Hedging FX Risk Management Techniques

The exporter can avoid FX exposure by using the simplest non-hedging technique: price the sale in a foreign currency. The exporter can then demand cash in advance, and the current spot market rate will determine the U.S. dollar value of the foreign proceeds. A spot transaction is when the exporter and the importer agree to pay using today's exchange rate and settle within two business days. Another non-hedging technique is to net out foreign currency receipts with foreign currency expenditures. For example, the U.S. exporter who exports in pesos to a buyer in Mexico may want to purchase supplies in pesos from a different Mexican trading partner. If the company's export and import transactions with Mexico are comparable in value, pesos are rarely converted into dollars, and FX risk is minimized. The risk is further reduced if those peso-denominated export and import transactions are conducted on a regular basis.

FX Forward Hedges

The most direct method of hedging FX risk is a forward contract, which enables the exporter to sell a set amount of foreign currency at a pre-agreed exchange rate with a delivery date from three days to one year into the future. For example, suppose U.S. goods are sold to a Japanese company for 125 million yen on 30-day terms and that the forward rate for "30-day yen" is 125 yen to the dollar. The U.S. exporter can eliminate FX exposure by contracting to deliver 125 million yen to his bank in 30 days in exchange for payment of $1 million dollars. Such a forward contract will ensure that the U.S. exporter can convert the 125 million yen into $1 million, regardless of what may happen to the dollar-yen exchange rate over the next 30 days.

However, if the Japanese buyer fails to pay on time, the U.S. exporter will be obligated to deliver 125 million yen in 30 days. Accordingly, when using forward contracts to hedge FX risk, U.S. exporters are advised to pick forward delivery dates conservatively. If the foreign currency is collected sooner, the exporter can hold on to it until the delivery date or can "swap" the old FX contract for a new one with a new delivery date at a minimal cost. Note that there are no fees or charges for forward contracts since the lender hopes to make a "spread" by buying at one price and selling to someone else at a higher price.

FX Options Hedges

If there is serious doubt about whether a foreign currency sale will actually be completed and collected by any particular date, an FX option may be worth considering. Under an FX option, the exporter or the option holder acquires the right, but not the obligation, to deliver an agreed amount of foreign currency to the lender in exchange for dollars at a specified rate on or before the expiration date of the option. As opposed to a forward contract, an FX option has an explicit fee, which is similar to a premium paid for an insurance policy. If the value of the foreign currency goes down, the exporter is protected from loss.

On the other hand, if the value of the foreign currency goes up significantly, the exporter can sell the option back to the lender or simply let it expire by selling the foreign currency on the spot market for more dollars than originally expected, but the fee would be forfeited. While FX options hedges provide a high degree of flexibility, they can be significantly more costly than FX forward hedges.

The Internationalist

www.internationalist.com